Contents

<u>Rule 2</u>..

<u>Rule 3</u>..

<u>The Confident Conqueror</u>.

Master of the Game:

A Modern Male's Guide to Sexual Conquest

By C.K. Murray

Similar works by C.K. Murray:

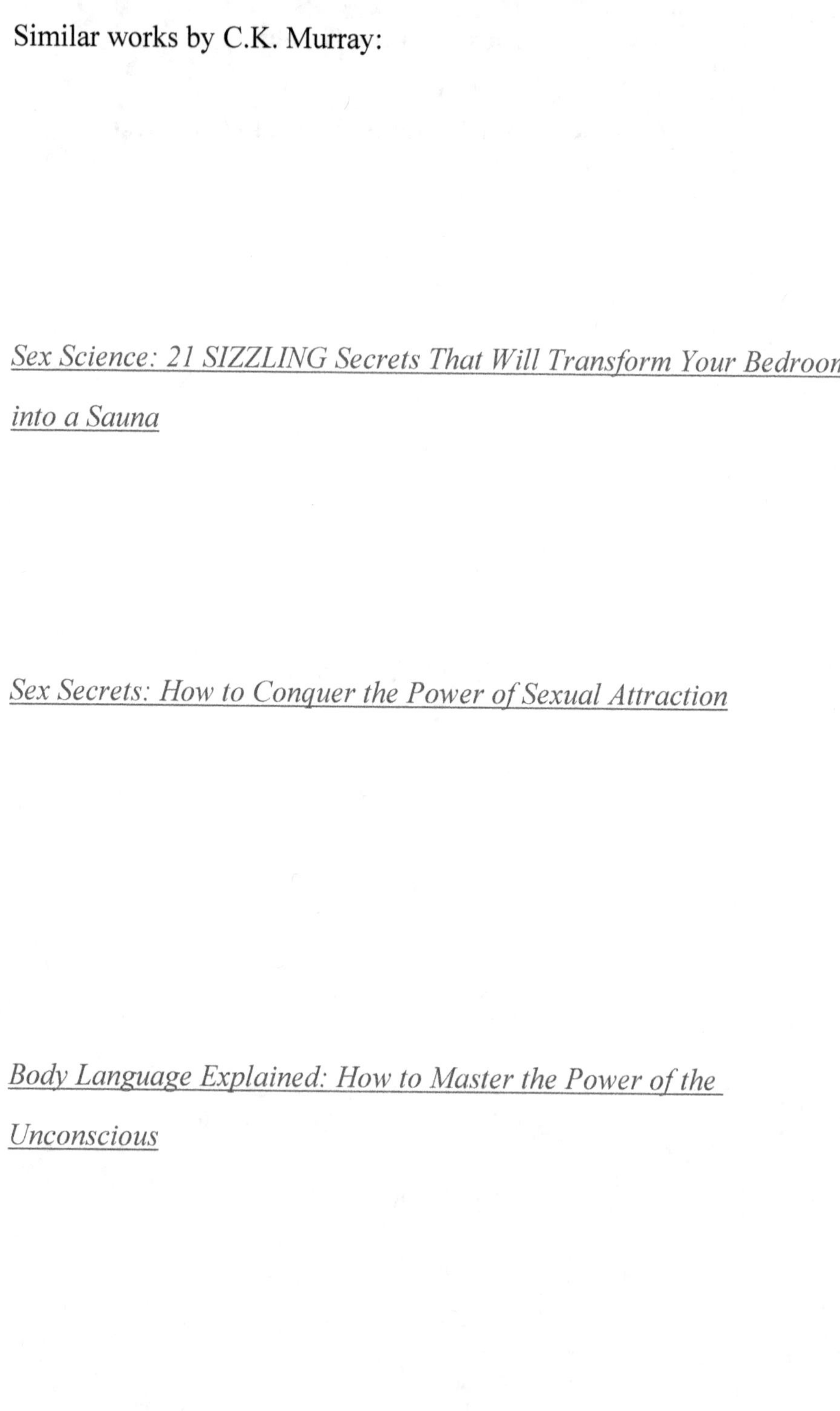

Sex Science: 21 SIZZLING Secrets That Will Transform Your Bedroom into a Sauna

Sex Secrets: How to Conquer the Power of Sexual Attraction

Body Language Explained: How to Master the Power of the Unconscious

<u>*Confidence Explained: A Quick Guide to the Powerful Effects of the Confident and Open Mind*</u>

Unlock Your Alpha

Gentlemen, the future is here.

We live in an age *saturated* with sexuality. Everywhere we walk, every nook, cranny and corner of this world and its virtual counterpart, is connected to sex. We are steeped in a life of sexual potential; molded by moments and opportunities for absolute *conquest.*

We are men of the night. Primal and predatory. Animals of appetite.

We are men of the day. Keen and connected. Exuding an aura that literally *restructures* the neurochemical properties of the female sex drive.

And they want it. Women—they *need* it.

So are you a man that can deliver? Are you a man of potential and power, the type of single male that can captivate females far and wide? The type of man that catches eyes, flutters hearts, and leaves damsels drooling at your every move?

Or are you lesser?

The woman of the modern paradigm is different. She is complex, she is powerful. She exercises her emotions, her libations, with freedom and fury. Her access to information is incredible; and so too, is her need for man.

But not just any man will do.

If we allow them, women can change us. They can turn us to subservient, mindless grunts. They can command us; they can *reprimand* us. And, most notably of all, they can possess our minds and hearts like nothing else.

The modern woman is a sexual being of tremendous power. But so too are we.

We live in a world *saturated* with sexuality. And today, that world is ours.

Gentlemen, let's Master the Game.

Know the Game

Unrestricted stimuli.

That is our world today. Everywhere we go, our technologies are reshaping our schemata, our perceptual framework for viewing this world. We zoom about on our smartphones, check our friends on Facebook and twitter and Instagram and Foursquare and a million other established networks and startup systems. We send our texts, stream our videos, change our schedules and power the pulse of modern progress.

And all the while, we forget an all-important truth: we're distracted. We've forgotten our power. We've lost it amid the haze. Which is why we need to change our ways. It is time to up our game to the next level.

But first, we need to *know* the game. If you don't know the rules, you'll go nowhere. You'll fret and fumble, struggling like all the others. You'll become nothing more than another meaningless part of the undifferentiated mass of ordinary suckers.

Is that what you want?

No, of course not—so let's cut to the chase. You're single, you're searching, you're ready to play. When you're out, you see them. Women everywhere, with their hair up and their hair down. With their stiletto heels and Estee Lauder lips. Lace panties and garter straps; bodies that curve like the crescent moon.

But how do you leave your footprint?

Easy, you follow the rules:

Rule 1 – Own It

What is "it," you ask? "It" is everything. It is you; you here, you there, in every spot you show your face. "It" is the aura that turns heads and locks eyes. "It" is the reason women want you, the reason their minds turn naughty when you step in the room. "It" is what you must find, and you won't find it till you've found yourself.

Who are you? Do you even know?

Imagine, for a second, that you're at the club. It's a Friday night, the lights are gleaming off scantily-clad beauties, the music is pounding, you've got a few Rum and Cokes in the system, but you're still standing there, too scared to make a move. Across the bar, a ridiculous-lookin dude with a Ren and Stimpy beanie and the DUMBEST outfit you've ever seen is doing his thing. And it's working.

Because he's grinding on cute little *thang* and she's lovin it. And all you can think is... "What does he have that I don't have?"

The answer?

"It."

And the answer is simple. Too simple. It's nothing. It's being YOU. As trite as it is to say, sometimes, you just GOTTA DO YOU. But what does this mean? Well, for one, it means forget about others. Not caring about superficial details (how slicked your hair is, a small blemish on your shirt, the weakening of your Deodorant, your lack of bulging pectorals) is where "it" starts.

It's about being older and mowing your lawn with the shirt off, with what wispy hair you've got left blowin in the breeze. It's about entering a new country and not feeling like a phony when you take a shot at speaking their language. Having "it" is about not being afraid to repel some to attract others. And it goes from there...

If you find things funny, be a goofball. Dance like a moron, undulate your hands like waves on a beach, draw the eyes of others who will laugh and point. Think of it this way: Even negative attention is better than no attention. And usually, other dudes will only point and make fun of you because they're insecure. Why are they insecure? They're insecure because they lack the courage to be themselves, to let loose, to "act a fool."

But having "it" doesn't just mean busting onto the dance floor. If you completely hate to dance, if that "just ain't you," go another route. Silence is "it" too. Some people like to chill. And if you like to chill, by all means, bring on the Ice Age, Baby. Let the eyes rove. <u>Body Language</u> is easier to read than we think.

The problem is, we pick up on signals most the time, signals that are undeniably strong. But then, we screw ourselves over. Unfortunately, humans have incredible brains, and when we use these brains, we overanalyze, overthink, and many times revert to self-doubting. Remember, "It" don't think. "It" do. If you're getting a vibe, go for it. "It" is in the present. "It" is Now and Always. "It" is always ready to seize the moment.

Men and women are attracted to each other. They are attracted to the natural physical, emotional, and mental components of a given member of the other sex. When a woman sees a guy that is trying to be something that he is not, she'll know.

The point is: BE NATURAL. Don't FORCE. If somebody doesn't like you for who you are, forget them. Call them a "hater," give them the cold shoulder, pop on the shades, and "oh-I-can't-see-you" them. Whatever.

"It" is about thinking you're awesome, thinking you're cool, thinking you're silly, odd, goofy, fat, thin, emotional, [INSERT ADJECTIVE HERE]. It's about thinking you're something AND being satisfied with that something. As those lotion commercials seem to say: Love the Skin You're In. And if a woman doesn't like you for you, forget her. Move on and make moves.

But if you can't, if you can't stomach the fact that a woman does not want you—if your heart cracks with the thought of rejection—it's because you're forgetting something. You're forgetting the second rule.

Rule 2 – Conquer

Possess her?

No.

Control her?

No.

Conquer her. See, the problem with most men is weakness. Every day, fumbling, mumbling weaklings crumble before beautiful women. They say the wrong thing, think the wrong way, and in a mere matter of moments, they've lost it.

But why? Why is it that these men fail?

I'll tell you why. Men fail because of one reason: the power reversal. They have relinquished their power to the female. They put the pussy on the altar and they kneel before it in desperate devotion.

The single man should never become a woman's subservient. A real man dominates a woman. <u>Sex science</u> shows this. A real man is mysterious. <u>The studies</u> don't lie: women are significantly more attracted to men who they are unsure about. That is to say, when a woman cannot readily tell if a man is into her, she thinks about him more. She ponders him. She wonders what she's lacking, *if* she's lacking, if the man spends any time thinking about her. See, when a guy serves on a woman hand-and-foot, he loses her respect. He becomes a puppet, a pansy. On the other hand, when a woman meets a man that clearly resists *everything* she wants, she becomes frustrated and eventually gives up. But if a man plays the middle, never crossing too far to any one side, never yielding entirely but not clearly denying the woman either—then the woman begins to think.

And as she thinks more, she comes to a conclusion. She *must* like him.

After all, why else wouldn't she be able to get him off her mind?

Women want a man who can make decisions. A man of willpower. A man who is confident in both his actions and his thoughts; a man whose body language resonates with power. Women want a man unlike most. Or so they think.

The truth is, most of us *can* be that man. But most of us are not. Most men are meek. A meek man is a man who pours himself completely into a woman's life and has nothing else going for him. This is not a man. This is a shell of a man. An emotionally underdeveloped creature. A boy.

When a man shows that he can do without a woman just fine, the woman will work harder to get his attention. Instead of the man chasing the woman, the woman will chase him!

When a man has conquered a woman, he is not enslaving her. In fact, conquering a woman is still chivalrous. What most men forget is that women *want* to be conquered.

Think about it.

Women seek to please us. And they want to.

Men are bigger, stronger. We're the protectors, the providers, the guides that steer women to safety when the chop is rough. Every man wants a woman who appreciates what he does. Women recognize this. It's the reason they get on their knees to please us. The reason they spread their legs for our pleasure. They want to reward us. They want to show us. And if *we* show them—our power—they'll worship it.

Rule 3 – See EVERYTHING

When it comes to women, we have to be a step ahead. We have to see them before they see us, recognize what they're going to do before even they do. Although this may seem like a tall order, it is much easier when we know where to look.

So where do we look, you ask?

Well, where do women strut their stuff? Where do gentle curves and plump lips and stark, sultry stretches of flesh tease our eyes and tempt our senses? What is the only place rife with the scent of sex, rife with estrogen, testosterone, and the comingling of humans reduced to their most lustful desires?

That's right, the bar scene.

And what better microcosm for intergender relations and interactions than the bar scene? You know, where club-bangers bring babes in droves, get morons fist-pumpin, and inevitably leave some 21-year-old hotshot spewing juicy McNuggets all over the bathroom floor?

When it comes to the bar, there are plenty of women (and men) that typically manifest. Typically, you'll see one or more of the following at bars, and by noting them and understanding them, you will dramatically improve your chances. If you can understand the <u>Bar Scene Typology</u>, you can understand how women act toward men. And, more importantly, how women *perceive* men.

So let's review, both the men of the bars (our competitors), and the women of the bars (our targets). If we can learn what to see, we'll know what to do. Let's do it:

1) THE BLOODHOUNDS: That's right, we've all seen 'em. And they've all seen us. Well, SMELLED us, more like it. THE BLOODHOUNDS are the guys that constantly have their sexdars turned to overload. They've got the crosshairs on anything with female organs. You might see them briefing from a distance, and then they swoop in, pack mentality on full display, cornering the hapless target.

These are the guys who surround an attractive girl at the bar from all conceivable angles, overworking her, throwing corny one-liners such as, "Your eyes are like moonlight," or, perhaps, "You're so breathtaking."

You see, because THE BLOODHOUNDS have no conception of failure, they will continue to come on strong, ignoring all signals that the female is disinterested, focused solely on her swath of flesh and scent of perfume. They will only stop when the woman flees or a friend frees her from their clutches. In these cases, THE BLOODHOUNDS will indiscriminately locate other targets.

Now, in rare cases there are female BLOODHOUNDS. But more often than not, their desperation is even more unappealing than their male counterparts'. If they happen to be hot and horny, consider yourself extremely lucky, gentlemen (assuming, of course, they aren't just tryin to share the clap).

2) The LONE WOLF: The LONE WOLF is everywhere. And if this persona is executed correctly, it can reap countless benefits. In males, the LONE WOLF typically occupies several forms. It may be a guy sitting with his rum and coke at a table or at the bar, or simply standing, leaning against something, his eyes scanning the scene for prospects. Now, in most cases the LONE WOLF is not a pedophile. So that's good.

The male LONE WOLF is oftentimes younger but can be older too. When effective, the LONE WOLF exudes a sort of dark mystery and graceful subtlety. He may catch countless female eyes across the bar, and may be located strategically so as to have free space around him where a female LONE WOLF or gaggle of girls can then move to for potential conversation

The LONE WOLF will use tactics such as cellphone-checking and T.V. watching to feign detachment, but really he is watching everything and everyone. The LONE WOLF may elicit comments from girls such as "he's cute" or "I wonder if he's by himself." The beauty of the LONE WOLF is, people wonder, why is this wolf alone? And if the cogs start moving, and the hypotheticals conjured are positive, then the male LONE WOLF stands to gain.

Unfortunately, the ineffective LONE WOLF will not achieve any of these things. He will want to SEEM uncaring and detached, and he will, to a fault. And as such, nobody will pay him heed, aside from the bartender who exploits this lonely soul for his charitable tipping.

This ineffective LONE WOLF may be an older man who has been coming to the same spot for years, searching for the love of his life. Or he may be a younger gent who just wants to fit in but doesn't know how. He may tell people that he enjoys being an outsider, but somewhere, deep down inside, he wants desperately to 'get it in.'

Now, the Female LONE WOLF is a special specimen as well. The successful female LONE WOLF will often draw Bloodhounds from far and wide. If she's good, she will be one of the few capable of dispelling unwanted Bloodhounds with silent treatment, vague responses, and blatant interest in other areas of the bar.

If interested in a suitor, the female LONE WOLF will be coy, seductive, often possessing an alluring control of her lips and eyes—a mesmerizing, understated confidence.

The ineffective female LONE WOLF may choose her isolation due to self-esteem issues, or may simply be having a bad day. In this case, she wants nothing more than to wash it all away, dreaming of meeting somebody, ANYBODY once heavy intoxication ensues.

An important distinction to make with LONE WOLVES is that all go with the intention of getting with somebody. Those who sporadically go to bars simply to have drinks after a long day or for reasons other than meeting other humans are not Lone Wolves. If these same people go to the bar regularly after work, and always claim they just "want to have a drink in peace," then they usually ARE Lone Wolves and are secretly looking for company.

3) THE OPRAH WINFREY: Everybody knows ORPAH WINFREY. She's revered 'round the world; she essentially owns the world. In terms of power, her nearest competitor is God.

Who else can buy cars for everybody in the audience?

In the bar, THE OPRAH WINFREY'S drinks are her cars. Oftentimes dressed to kill and exhibit wealth, but not always, THE OPRAH WINFREY has no problems blowing inordinate amounts of money in a single, binge-drinking night; night after night after night. THE OPRAH WINFREY is the guy or girl who somehow gets to the bar first, knows the bartender, gets served before people who have been waiting forever, and slides a credit card across the counter with the expected, "Keep it open" line.

THE OPRAH WINFREY is there to party and blow money, and she or he could not care less. They buy the shots, they get the rounds, and if you dare offer to pay or remark that they're spending haphazardly, they'll wave it off like it's nothing. Open that trust fund, baby!

THE OPRAH WINFREY usually doesn't have a game plan for hooking up with somebody, but more often than not, this person, what with such obvious wealth and uncaring attitude, will end up with several opportunities for 'partnership.'

However, many times, they'll get so blasted, they won't even know their own name by the end of the night, let alone that of the girl/guy they've been chatting it up with since Patron shot #6.

4) The EYECANDY: Everybody likes candy. It tastes sweet. And boy oh boy, does it look sweeter.

The EYECANDY is that girl or guy that sticks out like a rose in a briar bush. In female form, the EYECANDY is gorgeous. Oftentimes Barbie-doll like but sometimes (and this may be construed as 'disrespectful') they just look slutty. They wanna be noticed. They want guys to ogle their cleavage, to stare at their rump, to talk in hushed voices about their low-cut dress. They know they've got a body and they want everybody else to know it too.

The Female EYECANDY can be very smart or very dumb and bimbo-y. They might just like 'toying' with guys so that they can shoot them down in some form of twisted Neo-Feminism. They might enjoy playing hard-to-get, or they might, quite honestly, just be looking to get reamed (See: any porn video ever).

The female EYECANDY will oftentimes surround herself with a group of lesser attractive friends, just to make herself stick out even more. She will downplay her hotness, complement her friends on their alleged attractiveness, and act oblivious to the fact that she specifically and meticulously picked out her outfit to highlight her every prominent, jaw-dropping feature.

She has her friends to improve her self-esteem because ironically, due to her incredible looks, she may be quite insecure. Not always, but it definitely occurs.

On the dance floor, everybody watches her. As she walks by, everybody watches her. She has a syrupy sweet voice when she orders drinks, and so it's no surprise, she always gets served promptly. However, because she is so attractive, she often perpetuates her insecurity by scaring off potential suitors who can't muster the courage to approach her, lest they be labeled as 'lustful pigs.'

Then at the end of the night, as her lesser friends (friends she says she's happy for) are suckin face with brosephs, she's left wondering why she, the 'pretty one,' is going home alone.

The male EYECANDY is much the same. Sometimes metrosexual, sometimes Guido, or maybe just ruggedly handsome, the male EYECANDY knows girls want him. He's confident bordering on arrogant, and he sees women more or less as a means to an end. He may come with a pack of bros, all of whom glob to him for his incredible powers of female seduction, all of whom secretly aspire to be him.

He might be genuine friends with them, but when they enter the bar scene, their days of trading off high scores on Tetris mean nothing, and he will abandon the pack in a split second for any hottie he sets his eyes on.

He downplays his success, doesn't talk much about his 'game,' but deep within, he's constantly reminding himself how much of 'The Man' he really is.

He loves to play girls off of one another. Guys who don't know him (and many who do) think that he is manipulative and vile, and wonder aloud what it is that women see in him. The male EYECANDY is so set in his ways that half the time he doesn't even realize that what he is doing could be construed as immoral or sleazy. Or maybe he just doesn't give a hoot.

He believes that he is a superior creature, and that if he and a woman enjoy a night of lust, then so be it—the only thing he fears is a relationship.

By and large, he can do what he wants, and with his suave ways and startlingly good looks, he can talk his way out of almost any transgression.

He's always freshly showered, smelling of nice cologne, and always comes strapped for war—a condom in his back pocket.

Or maybe two.

He's the kind of guy that won't make a move on a single girl all night, then 20 minutes from closing time, can approach a hottie, seal the deal, and sexile his roommate, all with the flash of a smile and the wink of an eye. *"OMG, sooo hawwwt!"*

5) THE SHOCKER: That's right. And no, I'm not talkin about some lewd gesture or finger positioning. I'm talking about that guy or that girl who SHOCKS you. I can see your eyebrows scrunching in curiosity... Let me explain.

Let's start with the female version. The female SHOCKER is usually soft-spoken. She is cute and attractive and something about her seems to catch a lot of eyes. Though she is dressed rather modestly, her gentle, suggestive ways leave you wanting so much more. She doesn't wear much make-up, and she doesn't need to. And, despite her lack of revealing clothing, it's easy to see that her body is something great.

After a few drinks, she loosens up, and physical contact occurs. After a few more, she may depart and head to the dance floor. It is there, that she gradually works her way into rhythm. She is graceful and flexible, and she can undulate in ways that leave you intimidated before you've gravitated. Certain features that before were only partially discernible become alluringly apparent.

She will not plead you to dance with her, but her eyes flicking to yours, call you in. And so, chugging the last of your watered down Whiskey Sour, you join her.

If lucky, you take her home for the night. And that's when the real SHOCKER strikes.

Those same moves on the dance floor are amplified ten-fold beneath the sheets, and in embarrassment you find yourself struggling to endure. The girl who seemed so innocent and inexperienced at first glance, becomes the girl who's willing to try anything, in any position, sensual as all hell. She blows your mind, giggling and smiling, and she works your body like nobody before. You're blissfully shocked.

When all is said and done, she says she's fine with it being a 'no-strings-attached' affair. You find yourself wanting to date this girl. She's so sexy, so cute, so chill, so down for whatever. But softly, and respectfully, she informs you that it was just a night of fun. And like that, *that* is that.

The male version of THE SHOCKER comes in several varieties.

He may appear shy at first, but beneath that quite exterior is a booming confidence. He may even be dressed like a scrub or his clothes might not match, or it might appear that he has no style whatsoever. He doesn't want to fit in and he doesn't care if people think he's odd. He is attractive and he doesn't care to flaunt it.

When talking, he is adoringly awkward, and seems to have trouble establishing the first move. He may make several attempts at initial contact before succeeding or he may take a completely different approach, asking women straightforward, personal questions.

Normally, they would offend women or turn them off, but his odd, unexpected conversational style leaves them laughing and strangely drawn. Women find themselves liking his nerdiness, even wondering if he knows anything about women.

Once lured onto the dance floor, his idiosyncrasies wash away. He's able to mirror a girl's body movements, and he gradually changes the pace, moving her this way and that, working his hips and hands so that in time the two of them are practically sexing in clothes.

He squeezes her rump or rubs her inner thigh, but in the most non-threatening way, and she suddenly finds herself trusting this guy that she barely knows. His gentleness and sensitivity turn her on, and she can't help but love the nuances of his movements. Inevitably she finds herself wondering if that same sensuality carries over to the bedroom…

If they do go back to the bedroom, she finds out that, yes, it does. The SHOCKER might be that he is well-endowed. Or it might be that he can play her body like a flute. No matter his talents, he is a pleaser, and from giving her pleasure, he is able to turn himself on.

She finds herself having more of an emotional connection to him than she's ever had to any other 'fling'. It's because he doesn't mind spooning, and he can get his muscles contracting and expanding like nobody's business. He's a man of rhythm and grace, and *boy* does that get her toes curling.

6) THE STATEMENT: Look around you. Chances are, somebody's trying to make a statement. It may be a transsexual, a transvestite, a chick or guy with way too many visible body tattoos, a chick or guy blinged-out in medallions, or a wrinkly geezer 'doin the dougie' at a college kid's hotspot.

Most chicks dress provocatively at clubs and bars these days, so that can't be considered making a statement. Most dudes dress well to attract these well-dressed chicks, so that isn't really making a statement either.

THE STATEMENT draws appreciators and haters from all over. THE STATEMENT is a visual anomaly first and foremost, but, in rare cases, may deliver a multisensory overload.

Picture a wasted drinker protesting Medicare when he's not drumming on the bar counter to the antiquated Renaissance music in his head. Or maybe just a dirty, scraggly-haired dude straight from the dump yard, stinkin up an upscale DC bar with a cover charge of $50. If he managed to get in (unlikely), his intention is to draw attention.

In women, the STATEMENT may be inked to the max, dressed up like Lady Gaga, or full of vivid hair dye and strange piercings.

You'll know 'em if you see 'em.

7) THE BRUH

I'm not referring to guys that show up after work in their dress shirts, ties and slacks, nor am I talking about the 'bros' that rip shots of Jagermeister and scream "Whoooooo" all the way to black-out. I'm talking about the BRUH. The BRUH is a guy that has no plans, no obvious aspirations, no clear goal in attending the bar or club.

The BRUH is typically stoned upon arrival. He might be rockin sandals or loafers. He might have hemp necklaces or bracelets, and his eyes are bleary, reddened slits. He doesn't go out of his way to meet people, but they all seem to know him. He's easygoing and friendly, but only when somebody else initiates. Otherwise, he is content to just... chill.

Girls may be turned away from the BRUH because of his lack of 'life trajectory' and lackadaisical style. Or, girls could be attracted to him for these same reasons. Strange, but true.

These girls may be 'BRUHS' themselves. They might see in their male counterpart a certain tortured struggling artist. For many BRUHS, the tortured artist is buried deep within, but may come out in moments of guitar-strumming, bong-ripping, or conversations with small, trusted circles of friends.

All in all, the BRUH'S just tryin to chill. If you're not about it, that's cool. If you are about it, holla atchya boy or girl.

8) THE FRET

The FRET, like the name suggests, is worried about everything. He/she is fretting about how he/she's gonna get to the bar, where he/she's gonna sit, if he/she's been in one spot for too long, what he/she should get once he/she's at the bar, if a recent deposit went thru yet on the debit card, if he/she should try to talk to a girl/guy, if his or her collar is lookin sharp—you name it, the FRET is frettin

The FRET is that guy or chick that doesn't know what to do. This is the one that turns to a group of friends and says, "You wanna hit another bar?" This is the one that is already wondering how much a beer costs before taking a sip of the current drink.

The FRET might be a cokehead, but more often than not, the FRET is just a hyperactive malcontent who's always looking ahead ahead ahead ahead. Even as intoxication continues, the FRET is not satisfied. The Fret will simply become confused and confusing, disappearing to bathrooms, hollering at people for cigs, giving pats to acquaintances misinterpreted as 'friends.'

The FRET'S hyperactivity may lead him or her into sticky situations. A trusted guardian should watch the FRET to assure that the FRET doesn't run wildly into streets outside the club and get hit by a car or arrested by police or mugged by ruffians.

9) The TURTLE

We've all seen the Turtle. Imagine the Turtle as initially a shell. Then, a couple gin and tonics later, the Turtle emerges from its shell. And then it's something entirely different.

The TURTLE may manifest as a drunken floozy who normally spends her hours in the library but due to the bipolar shifting powers of alcohol, is now straddling everything with a schlong.

The TURTLE may be a guy who is usually calm and accepting, but suddenly morphs into a cantankerous, red-faced bully who finds himself shouting obscenities at passing vehicles.

The TURTLE may be a stressed, TYPE-A stroke-waiting-to-happen that after consuming his fair share, is goofy, giggly, and carefree.

The TURTLE may be a poor sob who after getting crunked, forgets his financial woes and blows money like a leaf blower blows... leaves.

The TURTLE is found in AAA meetings all over the world. The TURTLE is often encouraged by friends who find the drastic mood changes funny. For other friends, the mood swings are not funny. People may recommend psychiatric help. Oftentimes the TURTLE's life problems come spilling out at one point or the other when wasted.

However, it is important to realize that in some circumstances, the

TURTLE may completely fabricate things or 'admit' things that make no sense: "My father died in the Revolutionary war! I never got to tell him I loved him!"

The TURTLE may score girls or guys simply through his or her emotional outpourings. But usually, this requires the recipient of the outpourings to be equally intoxicated.

It does happen though.

10) The BAGGAGE

The BAGGAGE is the kid that nobody wanted to bring to the bar, but he or she came along anyway. This globule wanted to feel part of the group, but clearly has no idea what to do.

THE BAGGAGE don't grasp the bar scene, and will stand silently, oddly. He or she doesn't understand the dynamic. Worst of all THE BAGGAGE expects a drink to be purchased and delivered personally.

BAGGAGES have no idea how much drinks cost and when they actually do offer money to pay for their drink, they give way too little, and then, to make matters worse, they feign knowledge, saying something along the lines of, "that should cover it."

The BAGGAGE is usually somebody who is more comfortable at home watching T.V. or reading on a weekend night (which is fine). The only problem is, they become personally offended when not asked to come out, even though 98% of the time in the past they declined such offers.

The BAGGAGE will stand on the fringes of the dance floor when everybody else in his or her group is dancing. Others will feel bad, and may feel an obligation to 'babysit' or encourage the BAGGAGE to partake. Of course, the BAGGAGE will not assert him or herself one way or the other, and despite everybody's efforts, will not loosen up from the alcohol.

This is probably due to the fact that the BAGGAGE stops drinking after 2 or 3 drinks.

People do like the BAGGAGE. But in the bar or club setting, the BAGGAGE is an alien. The BAGGAGE has an esoteric knowledge of low-budget films, banned literature, and obscure facts. The BAGGAGE may share this oddball collection of goodies after drinking a few drinks. The BAGGAGE may have trouble recognizing that others in his or her group do not particularly care for such facts.

The BAGGAGE is not the best at social cues.

11) THE PET

The PET is more often seen at dinner parties or house parties, but is definitely present at bars as well. The PET is that powerless man or woman who is dragged, on a leash, to the place of drink and merriment. The PET is dragged by his or her girlfriend or boyfriend and does not want to be there. The PET may try to escape the clutches of its partner when at the bar, but the partner will maintain a firm hold.

The PET will be forced to get drinks and to meet all of its partner's friends and acquaintances. As a guy, the PET is typically looks like a starved weasel. He will be taciturn and will lower his head as he returns to the bartender at his larger girlfriend's bidding.

He will not stray from the girlfriend's hip until either drunk enough to have the courage, or when given permission. He will talk only about things that she likes, only when she's confident her friends won't perceive him wrongly.

The female PET will be equally dominated. She'll huddle by her man, saying nothing and doing nothing until her leash is extended. She will give scripted responses and introductions to her partner's friends. These scripted words will be planned carefully during the car ride to the bar.

She will not be allowed to divulge anything personal. The female PET's partner will want her to fetch drinks for everybody. She will be expected to do so promptly and agreeably.

After leaving the bar, the PET, male or female, will not be allowed to 'be themselves' until arriving home. Only then, may the PET's leash be removed, pending the partner's appraisal of the

PET's strengths and shortcomings of the night. If things go poorly, the PET may be punished and forced to sleep on the couch or pull-out.

If things go right, the PET will be expected to engage in doggy-style.

12) THE DUSTY DUO

Alright, alright, so they aren't necessarily "dusty" but they're definitely old. Well... older.

I refer to the couple, long-time married or at least 10+ years monogamous, that you see at the bar. They might go out to wine and dine with friends, but they always stick around till the owl hours. You'll spot them at college kid hotspots, kinda outta place, but also, quite frankly, kinda refreshing. Maybe they feel hip or alive when around younger kids. Maybe it brings them back to their days of folly and fornication.

Whatever. The point is, these smiling wrinkles are present, and not afraid to make that presence known. They might get sauced and start slow dancing, in front of everybody. Or they might strike up convos with the Youngins, applaud the drunken escapades of the Youngings, or even get all buddy-buddy with the bartender.

The DUSTY DUO has seen its share of trials and tribulations. They've lived through Woodstock, probly conceived a few kids in the fields— and they definitely aren't afraid to dredge up the ol' past. Once sauced, they'll tell cute girls "You look just like our daughter!" or exclaim to the young gents, "You look just like our son!" or "Tell me you're single? I'd love to match you up with my grandson!"

The DUSTY DUO may be looking to relive some old memories. They might reanimate at their wedding songs, or, to the surprise (and chagrin) of all, start break-dancing to the hottest and latest club-bangers. They might buy others shots just because they love to mix and mingle, and reminisce—"reminds me of the Manhattan Project!"

This DUO might consist of a woman with frizzy grey hair and a guy with a 70s porn stache. Or they might have updated their looks. Perhaps, they both went under the knife. Or maybe, they just aged gracefully.

It's always curious, in situations where the husband or wife temporarily disappears. The one partner may be off to the urinal, but the remaining partner at the barstool is suddenly bait: You'll see young guns tryin to swoon the milf or gilf. You might see voluptuous Juliets reaching for the silver hair of the distinguished man. And the best part is, there are no consequences. The partner will return and the DUO will get a hearty laugh. The suitor, of course, will be mortified, but nonetheless return to his or her friends to relate the odd turn of events.

13) THE TWO-FACE

A TWO-FACE is somebody with two faces. DUH!!

But in this case, the TWO-FACE is really two different types of people. Each one having, well, just one face. Let me explain:

In the bar scene, the TWO-FACE will be one of two people. Either, (A) the annoying skonz that always yells about being "so waaasted! I've had like 20 shotssss!!" or (B) the person that denies and hides intoxication at all costs, for reasons unknown.

This is the way it is.

The TWO-FACE may not drink anything. But will nonetheless feign drunkenness just to get attention. This is the person that hasn't grown up since high school when 'crushing' a six pack with buddies or killing wine coolers with 'the girlies' was so cool and so new. For whatever reason, the TWO-FACE still boasts of drinking to the point of needing the stomach pumped.

Black-out episodes are recalled in excruciating detail (which is hard to do given, the uh, supposed lack of consciousness at time of said episode).

The TWO-FACE will regale you with tales of every single day of drinking; stories of the most boring, depressing, pointless one-beer binges that you've ever heard. They tell their tales with so much gosh darn excitement, you'd think they won the freakin Lottery.

The TWO-FACE who gets fudruckered beyond belief but tries to disguise it, is equally perplexing. This individual will be that guy or girl walking really slowly, with blank, vacant eyes. He or she may have trouble responding and will take a long time before talking slowly. This is because he or she is struggling to organize thoughts and prevent slurring of words.

This TWO-FACE may speak of drinking obscene amounts, but will not brag. Instead, the achievements of gross consumption will be conveyed through nonchalant comments sprinkled here and there: "Yea. I had like 14 beers, I was fine tho. Drove home n all." This TWO-FACE will downplay intoxication and always volunteer to be the designated driver.

This TWO-FACE may be so used to denying intoxication that he or she will develop PILS (pronounced "pills"). That's Pathological Intoxicated Lying Syndrome. This TWO-FACE will talk to cops about being sober when in fact wasted. Unfortunately for the TWO-FACE, the drunk lying will become so engrained, it will become the truth in the TWO-FACE's mind.

--You just blew a .4, sir. We're gonna need to take you to the precinct.

--Whaaat? I'm fine! I'm sober as a bird!

The TWO-FACE views any drinking scenario as a time in which to exhibit awesomeness. Either awesomeness in terms of one's ability to guzzle and act unaffected, or in terms of one's ability to guzzle and get incredibly rowdy and saucy. These are the only two reasons. This is the dichotomy. That is all.

***

The Confident Conqueror

<u>Good</u>. Now you know. You are now aware of the three rules of The Game. Remember, nothing is better than face-to-face interaction. If you are trying to pick up a hottie, you need to <u>talk</u> to her! Real talk, not some meek "hello" followed by a Facebook friend request when you get home. Turn off your phone, stop following Instagram, stop listening to your Ipod, and approach that girl!

Obviously, Mastering The Game is all about confidence. We know that it's good to understand people. It's good to 'read' them. You need to know what's up. If you wanna pick up women, ladies, chicks, girls, babes, birds, bitches, chicas, hotties, floozies, sluts or shorties, you've gotta play the part. It doesn't take nanotechnology. It takes pep in your step and a willingness to fail.

In review:

- <u>TALK THE TALK</u>

Whether you're a poor sob, a rich widower, college kid, a Santa Claus look-a-like, a suave Guatemalan, a struggling actor, a computer programmer who's never seen the light of day—whatever your make and model, it's worth remembering:

IT AIN'T WHAT YOU SAY, IT'S HOW YOU SAY IT.

A million people have said it, but it's true. If you're merely a substitute teacher, don't go telling people "I'm a sub" with a shrug or a scowl. Tell them you "mold the minds of tomorrow." Exclaim that you're "an educator," that you're the favorite--how all the little girls and boys tug at your pant legs in love. And not in the Jerry Sandusky sense.

Don't talk through your nose. Don't sound like a whiny, driveling chicken bone. Nobody wants to see how life gets your trousers in a tussle. People don't want to see you breaking down or pitying yourself. Self-loathing is not attractive. Constant nervous laughter or fidgeting is not good. Don't have a squeaky voice. And don't talk like Zeus either. You're trying to get somebody in the sack, not get sacked in the face.

Tell people that you're 30 and you live at home. But remind them that you always keep the mini-fridge stocked. And that the entire basement is your domain. Make 'em know how comfortable the AC is. And in icy winters, the hearth is always glowing. And your parents won't bother outsiders so long as they don't track mud in the door and keep their voices soft.

Some people can make the greatest, most successful jobs sound like drudgery. Others can make pumping septic tanks sound grand. An individual with 'game' will poke fun at crappy jobs or make them seem important. Everything will sound novel and cool. Discussions of the mundane will turn into something that makes you pee your pants in anticipation.

·   <u>BODY LANGUAGE</u>

If a girl or guy craves another guy or girl, that individual will show it. Through body language, the individual can signal sexual attraction consciously and unconsciously.

<u>Guys must do this</u>:

Stick your chest out

Keep your shoulders back

Be relaxed

Take up space

Drape your arms over chair

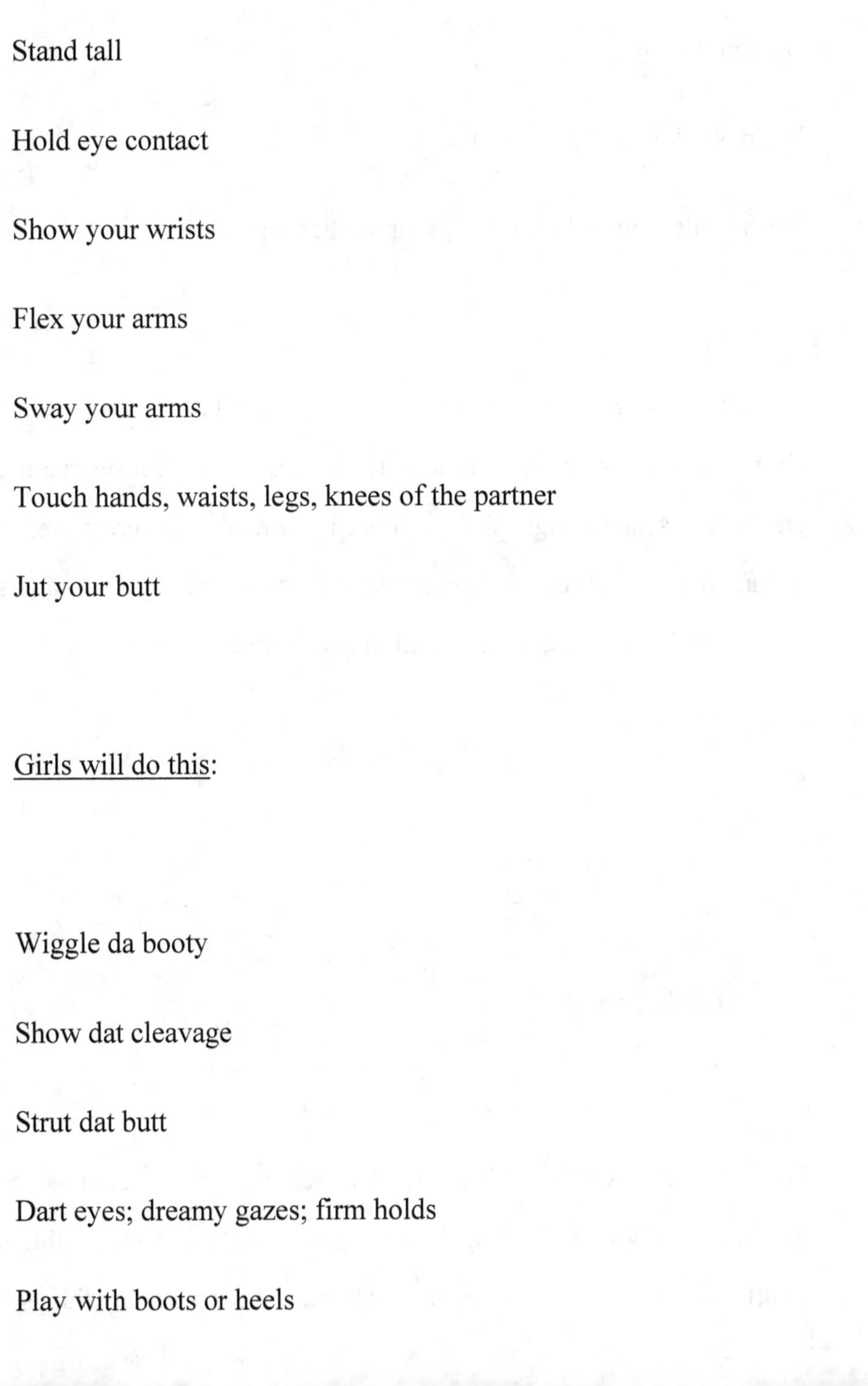

Don't cross your arms

Don't fidget or rub yourself

Stand tall

Hold eye contact

Show your wrists

Flex your arms

Sway your arms

Touch hands, waists, legs, knees of the partner

Jut your butt

<u>Girls will do this</u>:

Wiggle da booty

Show dat cleavage

Strut dat butt

Dart eyes; dreamy gazes; firm holds

Play with boots or heels

Cross legs

Expose thighs

Bump into guys

Whip, stroke, toss, play with hair

Flash smiles, purse lips, bite lips, apply lipstick

**A lot of the above things happen unconsciously. And a lot of things not mentioned also occur naturally. However, by consciously making an effort to send the right signs to those individuals of interest, we expand the lines of unspoken communication. Body language matters more than spoken language. Flirtation is engrained.

Get some.

· <u>FEARLESS</u>

We're humans. We fear trying hard at something, only to learn we're not good enough. We fear putting all our eggs in one basket and getting no return. This is normal. And healthy. After all, there are many things we, as humans, cannot know until we've put in the time and research. We're gonna fear the unknown until it's known, and then we still might fear it. Or, we'll never think of the unknown--because we believe that doing so might produce fear.

But if you're trying to score with a chick, dude, woman, man, grandfather or reanimated corpse, you can't have fear. Having fear in approaching a stranger will get you nowhere. You'll run through all your weaknesses, all the crummy hypotheticals--any way you could screw it up and come across as a total spastic nutball goonkhead. And this ain't good.

After all, you're gonna fail. You're gonna approach somebody and he or she is not going to want you (unless you're Johnny Depp or Angelina Jolie). Be prepared to get shot down. Don't overthink. Just go up, introduce, or 'accidentally' bump into the person. The best opportunity is when there is an opening and you can just slide in.

You talk to cashiers and waiters and people in passing that you've never met, right? You talk to your pediatrician and your physician, new customers and employees, friends of friends, mutual acquaintances— you name it!

You talk to all of these people, and do you always make a *huge* deal of it, or do you talk to them because they're people just like you?

So go ahead, just make small talk. Small talk is the gateway to big talk, which is the portal to body talk, which is the wormhole to mattress thumping.

Just say what comes to mind.

Don't sell out and try to be the smooth operator that you ain't. A lot of guides and self-helps will tell you that laying an amazing pick-up line is the way to go. This is false. Studies show that a simple hello or hi is the best way. Then, venture in with a brief question that draws attention to the current situation, context or circumstance. This is called the *impersonal, interrogative comment.*

If you're in a bar, you could simply ask "Pretty crowded in here, huh?" You could comment on the weather, you can draw attention to the band or music, the loudness, the lighting, the type of people that are around. Make it simple and make it harmless.

Just do you.

And don't fear. Remember, the first thing you want to do is signal interest. If you show that you like somebody, they are more likely to like you. Don't try to impress, just try to communicate. Treat a hot girl like you would an unattractive girl. Women may say they like being treated like a Queen, but this can be misleading. Women want to be treated nicely, sure. They want to know that they are liked and appreciated (as do men), and they want to know that they hold some status or value above other women—which is why you're talking to them and not others!

Still, saying they want to be treated like a Queen is misleading, because a lot of men will automatically subjugate themselves in this regard. This is a no-no. If a woman is a Queen, you are the King.

But let's forget all this royalty talk. The facts are simple. Master the Game and the game will reward you. Be patient, be fearless, and never, *never* stray away from the threat of failure. You can't grow as a man if you don't take risks and don't mess up.

So step up. Stay confident and stay committed.

It's time to Conquer.

***

A Special Note:

Thank you for reading "*Master of the Game: A Modern Male's Guide to Sexual Conquest.*" If you enjoyed reading this book and would like to be included on an email list for when similar content is available, feel free:

SUBSCRIBE

As always, thank you for reading.

And may you continue to live healthily and happily.

Sincerely,

C.K. Murray

Other works by C.K. Murray:

1. *Mindfulness Explained: The Mindful Solution to Stress, Depression, and Chronic Unhappiness*

2. *Emotional Intelligence Explained: How to Master Emotional Intelligence and Unlock Your True Ability*